GIDDY UP, ESTELLE!!

WE'VE GOTTA LOT OF LIVING TO DO!

RUTH WHEAT

ISBN: 9798878996983

DEDICATION

This book is dedicated to my precious mother, Kathleen Estelle Buras, my spunky grandmother, Ruth Estelle Ragazinsky, my aunt, Alice McDonald, my sisters Mary Helen Buras, Patti Kaye Jones and Susan Annette Pipkin, my sister-in-law, Elizabeth Buras, my daughters Ashlee Wilson and Chelsea Braun. Of these precious ones, Alice, Mary Helen, Patti Kaye, Elizabeth, Ashlee, and Chelsea are still with me. Ruth Estelle, Kathleen Estelle and Susan are spending eternity in the arms of our Heavenly Father.

ACKNOWLEDGMENTS

This book would not have happened if not for the support of my friends and family. To Buck Wheat, thank you for always supporting me in all of my adventures and for reading my books! To Belinda Hamilton, thank you for the amazing cover design and feedback on the book's content. To my sister Mary Helen Buras and my friend Sue Milam for reading this book from cover to cover and giving me valuable notes; and to Pat Gardner, Barbara Lundsford Allen, and Carolyn Clary for sharing your stories with me!

CONTENTS

1

INTRODUCTION

I started writing a book about choosing joy, one of my favorite approaches to life and then, my mind kept going to memories that brought me both joy AND pain. Then, I realized that I have lived a LOT of life and I've earned every wrinkle and gray hair (that you could see if I didn't color it!) on my head.

That thought catapulted me into the realization that I've got a ton of life to live ahead! And, I have a burning, God-given desire to share hope, laughter, and the determination to live each day with purpose, to all my sisters out there who are in the same stage of life that I'm in.

Have you ever heard the phrase, "60 is the new 40? I think someone coined that phrase so that all of us gals in our 60's and plus, would feel better about aging. This phrase simply means that there's a lot more life to live. I gave this some thought and took a mind journey back to my 40's. Whew! What a trip!

Now, don't get me wrong, I enjoyed my 40's, well at least most of it. I was a mom, wife, sister, friend, Sunday School teacher, an executive in the staffing industry, chief housekeeper, theater booster club member, costume maker and closet entrepreneur during that time, and frankly, I was exhausted!

Though I'm really grateful to be out of the costume making business (did I mention that I can't really sew?), there are some characteristics of my 40's that I'd like to keep. I loved the feeling of promise about looking towards the future. I enjoyed being engaged with people in activities that gave me joy. I loved being connected with my family and friends. I also appreciate the wisdom that I'd gained and the wonder of things that were to come. I am so blessed to have had all the experiences, both good and bad, in my life leading up to my 40's, and the years following them. What characteristics of your forties would you like to re-engage? How exciting it is to think that we can be 60, and then some, and enjoy our lives as if we were in our 40's?! Giddy up! Let's do it!

I turned 70 in January 2024. How can that be?! It seems like I was 16 yesterday! What a way to start a year!

Now, I look at my life through a different lens. One that is clearly designed to help me capture and savor every moment of my life and look for ways to make a difference in the lives of people who know me and those friends I haven't met yet.

I hope as you read this book, you'll experience the following:

- ❖ A snicker or two at some of the shenanigans I found myself in and perhaps a giggle as you reminisce about some of your own personal ones.

- ❖ Curiosity about seeking and fulfilling your purpose.

- ❖ The realization that we have lots of moments to live and the value of living them without worry.

- ❖ A sense of personal relevance and your value to the world.

- ❖ An understanding that experiencing joy is a choice!

- ❖ The knowledge that we were created in the image of God, our Father, and that He made you the wonderous woman you are, and

- ❖ Comfort in knowing that God's Got This!

Over the next few chapters, I offer some insights that have had an impact on my life.

I share the benefits of choosing joy and starting each day with a grateful heart, how to avoid negativity in your life, pursuing the desires of your heart, taking care of your body and soul and finally how to keep going with faithfulness. You'll also be introduced to women who share their stories to encourage you along the way.

As you read through the following chapters, choose those insights that make sense for you. You will notice some of the chapters will have note pages for you to use. I put them there so that you can have them handy to jot down your thoughts. I don't know about you, but at 70 I may forget something if I don't write it down! I hope you'll take advantage of them. Who knows, you may have a book in you!

Enjoy the read, sisters!

Love and laughter from my heart to yours,

Ruth Wheat

Daughter of Christ, Wife, Mother, "Mia", Sister, Friend, Bible Study Facilitator, Church Choir Member, Writer, Retreat Planner, and Cookie Baker!

2

THE STORY OF OUR LIVES

On the day you were born, you began the calling that God had for your life. Jeremiah 29:11 says, *"For I know the plans I have for you,"* declares the LORD, *"plans to prosper you and not to harm you, plans to give you hope and a future."*

This is one of my favorite verses, because it really speaks to my life having meaning and the responsibility that I have to live the purpose that He has given me.

Each of us and our life stories impact others. As we age, we are gathering more experiences and adventures. The timing could not be more perfect for us to share them with others. Our world is topsy turvey and looking for answers, often in the wrong places.

It's not necessary to write a book, although it's a fun thing to do. What is necessary is to share your experiences when opportunities arise. Be sure to share both the good and the bad. God certainly works through both.

There are so many younger women who could benefit from a friend, a confidant, a mentor. As you take a stroll through your life, look for opportunities that you might be able to make a difference in another woman's life. You'll be amazed at the opportunities God will bring your way.

Over the next few chapters, I will be sharing some of my life story and hope that you will find it helpful and get a chuckle or two. I will also be sharing some stories of amazing women that I have met that had an impact on me.

Before we dive into my story, take a few minutes to jot down some memories that you'd like to share. The following page will give you some food for thought and a place to write.

Giddy up!

My favorite happy memories:

My painful memories:

What I learned through these experiences:

How can my experiences help other women?

3

ONE OF FIVE

January 22, 1954, was quite the day! My mother and grandmother were out inviting people to come to our church when a car plowed into the passenger seat, throwing my pregnant mom into a sea of traffic! My grandmother jumped out of the car to get help and comfort my mom. Taken by ambulance to Hermann Hospital, my mom found herself about to deliver and she wasn't ready! I wasn't due for another 4 weeks! All the plans had been made, but none included the car accident.

My grandmother finally sat down with the family in the waiting room and realized, she held her Bible in her hand. She didn't remember taking it out of the car, but there it was in her hand. Her immediate instinct was to grab something precious to her as she exited the car, God's Word.

Labor was difficult and the doctor came out and told my dad that there was a chance that either my mom or I might not make it. And, as with any difficulty my family was facing, they began to pray.

The next time the doctor came out to speak to the family, he introduced me to them and gave them the good news that my mom was doing great! My dad said my eyes were wide open and I looked like I was ready to tackle the world! I sure like to think about being "prayed into" this world!

In the years that followed, my parents brought three sisters, Mary Helen, Patti Kaye, and Susan, and one brother, Kenneth into the world. And, just like that, I was the oldest.

As one of five, I learned a lot - here goes: (Oh, can I get an AMEN if you learned any of these lessons, too?)

Lesson One -Five kids are a lot! And there was not always a lot of money to go around. But our dad worked hard, and Mom did her best to stretch the life out of clothes and meals. I learned to share, and as the oldest, to wait for others to get their share. What a blessing! I learned that giving to others was a good thing, though sometimes, I really wanted to grab a piece of the chocolate pie first! With 5 kids, you just never knew what was going to be left!

Lesson Two - "Going first", as my sister Mary Helen calls being the oldest, is not always easy! When I was about 12 years old, **all** of my friends were shaving their legs. Naturally, I wanted to have smooth, beautiful legs like my friends, but there was one problem. I didn't own a razor! I worked up all my courage to ask my mom if I could use her razor to shave my legs.

After what seemed to be hours (probably about 5 minutes) of

begging my mom, she gave in. Fortunately, I was the only one with her at the time and didn't have to face embarrassment in front of my siblings. That was until my mom called out to me as I went upstairs, to be to be careful shaving and to avoid cutting myself! This experience soon became the talk of the family!

Learning to go first, though, really served me in my life. I learned that some risks were worth taking and the thrill of doing something new was cool!

Lesson Three – Routines are necessary to keep the business of life organized. There were a lot of routines at our house such as everyone writing their name on a paper cup and keeping it all day! This saved a few pennies, and my mom was all about that!

And there were dishes that were to be done as soon as dinner was over so as not to have a messy kitchen. The worst part about that routine was that my sisters and I had to do it! And no dishwasher! I tell you what, even though I didn't like doing the dishes, I learned that a clean kitchen really made the house sparkle. And it's really a good feeling to finish something right. This lesson really served me well!

Lesson Four – It takes leadership to get your siblings to buy into your ideas! My sisters and brother probably thought I was being bossy. Well, maybe in some instances, I was. (Actually, I was quite good at bossy!)

Summer was always a cherished time of year because we were out of school. Mom would keep other children to bring in some extra income, so we usually had two or more extra kids that kept us busy.

Our street was filled with families with children our age, so we always had a bunch of kids to play with. One day, I decided that we had enough people to do a play. We came up with a story we all knew, and as the self-appointed director, I gave each kiddo a part to play. Our front yard was the stage because there was no way my mom wanted all those kids in the house! We practiced, made some costumes and it was time to perform. We went to our neighbors' houses, invited them to the play and gave them the "ticket" price. Lo and behold, we had a good crowd!

I learned two key lessons that day- if you give people an opportunity to be successful, they will buy into your vision. Leadership is not about being the boss, it's about engaging others and giving them opportunities to use their talents. I also learned that people love to support one another - sometimes you just need to ask.

Lesson Five - Having faith in God is the hallmark to a life worth living. We were brought up in a Baptist church. Our dad was a deacon and Mom taught Sunday School. We were at church every time the doors were open. And, while being in church was important, watching the lives of my parents and grandparents gave us the opportunity to watch faith in action.

Every night before we went to bed, our parents had us all kneel around their bed to say our prayers. I learned that making prayer an important part of your daily life was significant. Before we prayed, we had the "Bible Reading." Dad would read passages of scripture every night to a crowd of six.

Sometimes, I confess, my mind wandered a time or two, or three. But I learned that having a time devoted to prayer and Bible study was important to everyone in the family and would build a solid life foundation.

Lesson Six – We never know what we can do until we are put into situations that require us to do Herculean things. Eleanor Roosevelt's quote really sums this up... "A woman is like a teabag. You never know how strong she is until she gets into hot water!" I observed this in action when my parents divorced. Even though we were a strong Christian family, my parent's marriage ended.

I watched my mother move into a completely different situation than she was accustomed to. She had started working as an EKG technician a couple of years before the divorce. Mom had only started driving within that time frame, too. Working outside the home, driving, and raising five kids on her own was an experience that she certainly hadn't counted on. But she did it! She raised amazing kids and rose up the ranks in the hospital to become head of the outpatient facility.

Mom was my hero! I watched her tackle all kinds of new challenges with grace and determination. If she were here today and you asked her how she was able to move forward through such a difficult situation, she'd tell you God was her strength. He oversaw the details. He wanted what was best for her and her children.

The greatest lesson during this time of my life was the realization that we can be blind sighted by major events and when we feel like the world is swallowing us up, God is there to pick up the pieces help us put our lives back together.

There are so many lessons learned but such little time to share. I hope joining me in some of my memories will challenge you to give yourself the gift of going down your own memory lane. Jot down some of your favorite memories and lessons learned. It will do your heart good!

So, those of us in our 60's have lived over 21 thousand days. That's a lot of opportunities for lessons learned! We know a lot of stuff girls! Let's take every opportunity to share our experiences and be mentors for younger women to help guide and support them when they are needed.

4

LIFE IS A CHARCUTERIE BOARD

Charcuterie boards are all the rage! It's rare to go to a party or a luncheon without seeing one. They are found in all shapes and sizes, filled with delicious meats, cheeses, condiments and vegetables. I've seen some with vegetables resembling flowers! Just beautiful!

These boards are a delight to see and delicious to eat! As we look at all the wonderful treats awaiting us, we choose those that we enjoy the most or, in some cases, want to try for the first time.

I think life is like this. We have so many options to choose from some familiar and some new. Our beliefs and experiences can limit us from trying something new and can have an impact on living full lives. But you know what? We're in our 60's plus, and we have earned the right to do something new! And we should!

For example, I decided that I really wanted to try being a red head. I have a lot of freckles and I think gals with red hair and freckles are so cute! I bought a red wig when I was 60 and whenever I get the desire to go red, I do! How fun is that?!

Though trying something new can be exhilarating, it can also be intimidating. You may have experienced this, as I have at certain points in my life. Why? I believe that fear plays a big role here. It's natural to be cautious when looking at doing something new. But sometimes, our fears may cause thoughts that keep us from moving forward, even though the new adventure is just what we need.

Here are some thoughts that have entered my mind:

- ❖ "I've tried this before and it didn't work! I sure don't want to be a failure!"

- ❖ "What will people think? I don't want anyone to think I'm crazy!"

- ❖ "Looks interesting, but I'm not sure how to begin. It may take more time and effort than I want to commit to."

- ❖ "I'll get to it one of these days."

Do any of these statements sound familiar to you? If we're not careful, they can stop us in our tracks, and we may miss a great adventure.

You know, these experiences or changes that we are considering don't necessarily have to be life altering. For example, you may want to simply try a new hairdo. I mentioned earlier that I've colored my hair since I was in my 40's. As I contemplated turning 70, I gave a LOT of thought to doing something different with my hair. Maybe letting a little gray shine through would be a good idea. Or maybe I should let it grow a bit longer. It could be fun to make a change.

I suspect you may attack decisions like this by getting feedback from your friends and family. So, I launched my "hair input" campaign and received a lot of responses. Even Buck weighed in! He said, "Honey, I will think you are beautiful no matter what you do! And, if you don't like it, you can always change it!" (Have I mentioned how much I love this man?!)

I went to see my stylist this week. After I shared my thoughts, she suggested that we take it slow and use both blond and gray highlights in my hair and then go from there. You know what? I love it! The best part of this experience is that I learned that I don't have to always dive in headfirst. I can put my toe in the water and make a small change and see how it goes.

We can't fast forward our lives to see how things turn out, and honestly, I really don't want to know. But I do know that I want to live every single minute of it with all the gusto I can. This desire propels me to get past my fears and try new things. One of my favorite verses that helps me move forward is Psalms 34:4, "*I sought the Lord, and He answered me; and delivered me from all my fears.*" It's a comfort to know that our Father not only hears our fears, He knows before we ask.

What are some experiences that you've seen on "Life's Chacuterie Board" that have captured your attention? What are some changes you've considered? List your thoughts below and then consider what's keeping you from moving forward.

Life's Chacuterie Board

Some risks may seem scary, but the reward can be a huge blessing!

Giddy up, Sister!

5

"SURPRISE!"

I never thought I'd celebrate being in my 70's but here I am! I entered my 60's divorced, and on my own. I was embarrassed. Most of my friends in their 60's that were married were spending their "golden years" together. I had to pull up my big girl panties and move forward. Though a bit anxious, I knew that God had designed my future, and I was willing, nervous and a bit excited, to see what was next.

I had no idea what God had in store for me! My expectations were that I would work until my 70's and stay single. I loved getting up every day and going to work, so there was no reason to retire before then. Until God sent me Buck.

I was having lunch with a dear friend, and he suggested that I wasn't meant to be single. That I needed to get "out there". I just laughed! I was 62 for heaven's sake! He encouraged me to just try online dating, assuring me that this would be good for me. I have a habit of listening to my friends, and this sounded a little exciting. So, I dove in with both feet!

Sisters, let me tell you, the hardest part of setting up my profile was to figure out how to describe myself! I mean, how in the world could I share the "right" personal traits? You know, the ones that when read, the guy thinks "Oh my gosh! She's just perfect!" I was pretty sure that the fact that I considered myself a great crafter, loved to read mystery books, and enjoyed shopping were not the qualities that the man of my dreams was looking for! I must tell you, that's a lot of pressure!

I joined Match.com and set up a profile. I decided that my profile really had to "be me"! So, I included pictures of me with my grandson, speaking to a large group of people, wearing reindeer ears with my sisters and my vision board. I thought, "That should do it!"

To keep this short, I'll just say that I attracted a lot of attention, but to no avail. After my 90-day subscription was nearing its end, I decided to cancel. Sadly, I met a lot of frogs, but no prince!

On my last day, a guy named T.L. Wheat III, also known as Buck, (that's right! Buck Wheat) sent me a message through the service. He mentioned that he was very interested in my profile and would like to take me to dinner. I looked at his profile and he was **very** cute and looked like he was "safe", so I said yes.

We met for dinner and the rest is history. I met Buck, the love of my life, online when I was 62 and we got married the year I turned 64! I share this story for a couple of reasons. One, you are never too old to find love. You just need the courage to try. Second, marrying Buck was in God's master plan for me. I was on the last day of my subscription, ready to give up, and Buck found me.

Actually, Buck finding me was a bit of a miracle! He restricted his dating profile to only women who lived within a 5-mile radius of his zip code! I had just moved within that radius four months before! God's definitely in charge of the details!

This wonderful experience catapulted me into a different life, one with life-changing events that brought me here sharing my thoughts with you.

You know how you think you have life all planned? Sometimes it can take a turn and point you in a completely different direction. I was comfortably ensconced in Houston TX, with great shopping, lots of activities, and all of my family and friends close by. Buck was very supportive of my career and my desire to keep working, even though he had retired from his dental practice.

We decided to buy a vacation home so that we could enjoy getting away. I'd always dreamed about owning beach front property, so I was super excited. Well, as it turned out, we bought a log home in the Sam Houston National Forest! And, just like that, the beach house dream was gone. What I wanted and what God had planned were very different. And, so much better!

Now, I'm quite the city girl, so I never had a log home on my radar or my vision board! God surprised me again! Our vacation home was in the forest surrounded by wonderful Christian neighbors, on again-off again TV and phone service, and a view of the lake. We loved it so much that we moved to Huntsville TX full-time. This city girl loves the country! Who knew?

In this beautiful neighborhood, I am a co-facilitator of a ladies Bible Study and found lifelong sister friends! Another beautiful surprise!

I wonder what God has in store for you. Have faith! Be open to new things and step into them as He unfolds the path.

6

CHOOSE JOY

I grew up going to Sunday School every Sunday. There are many moments and teachings I remember, but one little song, "Joy in My Heart" by George William Cooke, set me on a lifelong path of choosing joy. Here are the words to the first two stanzas.

I have the joy, joy, joy, joy down in my heart,
Where?
Down in my heart!
Where?
Down in my heart!
I have the joy, joy, joy, joy down in my heart,
Down in my heart to stay.

And I'm so happy, so very happy,
I have the love of Jesus in my heart, down in my heart,
And I'm so happy, so very happy,
I have the love of Jesus in my heart!

I have a strong belief that my relationship with God is the foundation of my joy. But life can get messy sometimes leaving us to feel bombarded by negativity from a lot of different directions. I believe that we can choose how we react to both positive and negative situations.

The moment we open our eyes each morning, we get to begin a whole new day. No matter what happened the previous day, we are given a "do over." I consciously choose to be joyful. Once that decision is made, then my frame of mind changes and I look for opportunities to be joyful. This sounds simple, but some days may be more difficult than others.

It has always been my way to share the notion of choosing joy with people at work. Seems, they took notice and expected to see my joyful spirit every day. But on one particularly tough day when everything seemed to go wrong, one of my colleagues noticed something was up. He asked me, "Have you found your joy today?" I realized that I had not and said, "I haven't yet, but I will!"

Several other times during that day he stopped me and asked the same question. My response was the same. It was a rough day! But because my friend loved me enough to encourage me I found joy! Even finding joy later in the day made a difference.

The opposite is true if we choose anxiety, self-pity, anger, sadness and so on. I know that when we are aging, we encounter all kinds of situations that are hard to overcome. Just in the past four years, Buck has had a stroke, I had colon surgery, Buck's appendix ruptured, and I had a repair on a knee replacement that resulted in 6 months of heavy-duty antibiotics. Sadly, we lost Buck's mom, my precious sister, and my mom. Whew! That's a lot, but here's the really good part that happened within these four years. Buck and I got married!

These kinds of events seem unsurmountable and tend to bring sadness, the opposite of joy. We must find joy, even in the tough times. Choosing joy may mean celebrating only a moment. For example, you may receive a Facebook video of a precious grandchild swinging, or a phone call from a friend. These moments bring joy!

Whether we choose joy or not will have a direct impact on how we close our day, either happy, or stressed out. And these feelings have a direct impact on our ability to get good rest through the night, something critical to our health and well-being.

Let's dig a little deeper into joy.

What is Joy

We've heard this word so many times, but do we really know what true joy is? We know it when we experience it. I'm sure the feeling is different for everyone. For me, I feel lighter on the inside and depending upon the situation, my heart feels like it could burst!

Joy is a state of being. We often equate happiness to joy. But happiness is different in that it is driven by circumstances. Have you ever thought,

- ❖ "If I could just do...then I would be happy." or
- ❖ "I'll be happy when I lose 10 pounds!" How about this one,
- ❖ "If my house was bigger, or I had more storage, I'd be so happy!"
- ❖ If I had the right man in my life, I'd be so happy!
- ❖ "If I didn't have so many aches and pains, then I could do more!"

These statements reflect some of the conditions that we put on being happy. If we could catch ourselves doing this, then we'd see that our happiness is totally dependent on someone or something. I don't know about you, but I really don't want my happiness to be contingent on my circumstances.

Far too often, happiness is based on earthly experiences such as eating at your favorite restaurant, going on a great vacation, or material possessions whether it be getting the perfect dress for a party or a new car.

Another way to look at this is that happiness is outward, while joy is inward. Joy is based upon spiritual experiences, like caring for someone without expecting anything in return, and gratefulness for all the blessings in our lives.

Based on Webster's definition of joy, "a passion or emotion of gladness, exhilaration of spirit, delight." we can experience joy even when we aren't happy with our circumstances.

I observed this notion firsthand. My youngest sister, Susan, was diagnosed with colon cancer in her late fifties. A devoted Christian wife and mother, she was pure sunshine! What a joy she was to be around! I'll admit, I was angry when I learned she had cancer! How could that be?!

I watched Susan experience all of the side effects of cancer. Her hair was thinning. She lost her appetite; she was in so much pain that the only comfortable position was to lay on her back on the floor. I saw the sadness in her eyes as she looked at herself in the mirror. She had lost so much weight that she no longer wanted to see her image. There were some dark days when I didn't feel joy or gratitude. I was so broken hearted as I watched her suffer. I'll tell you one thing that still amazes me today; if Susan was angry, I never saw it.

During her illness she accepted that this was a season in her life. She found joy in her relationship with Jesus Christ and her family, even though she didn't have the energy to do much. She lived less than a year after she was diagnosed. Susan left this world of pain and discomfort and entered the gates of Heaven. We could imagine that when she saw Jesus, she threw her arms around his neck and thanked him for the life he gave her. Such joy!

At a certain point in our lives, our bodies may slow down, and we may be unable to do some of the things we used to. This is when it is especially important to choose joy in the things we CAN do.

Joy, most importantly, is based upon the Holy Spirit that lives within us as a believer. We can rejoice in all circumstances because God is with us every day of our lives, He will never leave us, and His peace fills us with calm. His joy gives us the strength to face negative circumstances with courage and grace.

Illustrations of Joy

Mother Theresa, the world-famous Catholic nun, is such an inspiration to me! Mother Teresa, when in her 40's, by the way, founded the Order of the Missionaries of Charity, a Roman Catholic congregation of women dedicated to the poor, particularly to those in India. They opened numerous centers serving the blind, the aged, and the disabled. Most of Mother Theresa's work was done in India. We can only imagine the level of poverty and disease that surrounded her daily.

One of my favorite stories about her is the day a reporter came looking for her. Everyone he met told him that he would find her cleaning toilets! And he did! She assumed when she saw him that he was there to help clean the toilets and gave him an impromptu lesson on how to do it properly. With all the suffering around her, Mother Theresa found joy in cleaning toilets! She said this about her work...

"Lord, give me this seeing faith, then my work will never be monotonous. I will find joy in humoring the fancies and gratifying the wishes of all poor sufferers. O beloved sick, how doubly dear you are to me, when you personify Christ; and what a privilege is mine to be allowed to tend you."

Consider this – Mother Teresa retired when she was 87!

Take Steps Toward Joy

I have a dear friend that quotes this scripture before she rises each morning, *"This is the day that the Lord hath made, we will rejoice and be glad in it!"* Psalms 118:24.

Another way to get into a joyful state of mind is to offer a prayer of praise to our Father. Name ALL your blessings as you pray, it may take a while! It is sure to make you feel joyful. In fact, how can you not feel joyful if you are focused on what God is doing in your life. What a great way to begin your day!

In addition to deepening your relationship to God, there are also some practical activities that I believe can add to your joy. Here are a few of them.

Make self-care part of your routine – As women, we often put everyone else's needs ahead of our own. I'm a wife, mother, and grandmother. I held executive positions in my career. I was responsible for the success of the company and the welfare of our people. So, I get it. There were many days that ended in my exhaustion. I eventually learned that the only way that I could follow my heart and help others, was to take care of ME.

One of the best analogies of self-care comes from the speech we hear preparing to take off in an airplane. The flight attendant tells us that in the event of an emergency we are to put our mask on first, and then attend to our children. It makes sense, doesn't it? If we take care of ourselves first, we can be who we need to be for others.

You're probably thinking, when do I have time for me?! You may find that it's best to get up early in the morning before everyone else for some "me" time. Take a walk, listen to your favorite music, take a fabulous bath, savor a cup of coffee, read your Bible, and pray. Just think about how you'll walk into your day if you give in to one of these ideas. For heaven's sake, don't choose to do the laundry, pick up toys, do the dishes, etc. When you choose to do these things, your mind is telling you that these things are more important than you. And your life can quickly be consumed with all of these "things."

When I retired, I thought that I was going to be bored and that I would just sit around watching TV. I'm one of those gals who gets involved with both feet! I love engaging with all my friends, and spending time with my sweet husband, but I need to take time for me too. So, I find time to read my Bible, pray, write, check on my friends on Facebook, etc. It may only be about 15 to 30 minutes, but it is lovely!

I'm going to challenge you to find 10 or 15 minutes a day to focus on YOU! Make it special. Find a spot that is just perfect for you. You may not have extra space so, take something special into the place you do have. I have a dear friend who took a small room in her home and turned it into her version of a "she shed". It's beautiful. She even has a small chandelier hanging from her ceiling. She goes in there to pray, read, sing, whatever her heart desires. She loves it!

One of my prized possessions is a coffee cup that one of my dearest friends gave me. It's pink with a tiny touch of gold and it says, "You're the sister I got to choose!" This cup, filled with hazelnut coffee or cinnamon tea is with me in my favorite space, It's a treat! How are you treating yourself?

Remember, we are given a fresh start every day. Think of all the things that bring you joy and immerse yourself in them. Make a conscious choice before you get moving, to choose joy! Once you make choosing joy a priority, you will be surprised at how quickly it becomes a natural lifestyle. This quote by Henri Nouwen sums this up. "Joy doesn't simply happen to us. We have to choose joy and keep choosing it every day."

What are some things that bring you joy? Jot them down – it will do your heart good!

Doesn't that feel great! Now, make sure you're getting a good dose of these things that you've listed in your life and choose joy every day!

Now grab a cup of coffee or tea and let's go to the next chapter. It's a doozie!

7

LOOK ON THE BRIGHT SIDE!

Wow! This is a tough one! Sometimes the bright side doesn't seem achievable because of worry. My guess is that by the time we hit our 60's we have done a lifetime of worrying! In fact, we women must have an extra gene in our DNA that makes us worry!

Oh, my goodness! We worry about everything! Moms and grandmothers worry about their children and grandchildren – their day to day lives, their health, etc. We worry about the state of the world we live in. Believe me, there's a lot going on there.

I've worried about things such as my healing from a back injury and my whether my daughter Ashlee's fertility problems would prohibit her from having a baby. (Praise God, she has two boys!)

Smaller worries, such as my grandson winning a tennis match or whether the girl he likes will go to a dance with him have also weighed on my heart. I'm afraid I'm one of those protective grandmothers.

And then the silly worries, like about whether a new casserole I've made will be well received can cause me to fret. For heaven's sake (as my grandmother would say)!

As we age, we worry about our health, and in some cases, we find ourselves caring for others who may be experiencing poor health. Let's face it, we can spend a lot of time worrying.

My mom, Kathleen Buras, would say to me, "Ruth, quit borrowing trouble!" She was right! Worry has a negative effect on our bodies. It is one of the big causes of stress. The Mayo clinic wrote an article on stress, listing these as some common effects of stress - headaches, muscle tension or pain, fatigue, stomach upset, and lack of sleep. It stands to reason that there is **nothing positive** about worry.

I ran across this wonderful quote by an unknown author. "Worrying won't stop the bad stuff from happening. It just stops you from enjoying the good." I wonder how much of the "good" we miss because of all our worry. It certainly steals our joy!

So how do we stop? I'm going to share a couple of ideas. The most important thing to do is to turn our worries over to God.

Lean on Jesus

In Philippians 4:6-7 we are given this promise. *"Do not be anxious about anything, but in every situation, by prayer and petition, with thanksgiving, present your requests to God. And the peace of God, which transcends all understanding, will guard your hearts and your minds in*

Christ Jesus." This scripture reminds us not to be anxious about ANYTHING! Amazing! We need to find a way to eliminate this anxiety in our lives.

"Let go and let God" is a phrase that is used among fellow Christians when offering hope of a new tomorrow and as a gameplan for giving God those things in your life that only He can handle. The phrase indicates two steps. The first is "Let go". This is not easy. One of my greatest flaws is the need to be in control, so this is a hard step for me.

My daughter had back surgery when she was 27. She was a young mother with a 2-year-old son. I was scared to death! Her husband and I joined her as she was admitted to the hospital. During the registration, she was asked if she would like a private or semi-private room. Because their insurance would not pay for a private room, they opted for the semi-private.

Now, the first thing that came to my mind was that I could pay the difference between the cost of the rooms. After all, I could afford it and I'd feel a lot better about things. Just as I was ready to open my mouth to speak, God stopped me.

He planted the idea in my mind that I needed to discover why a private room was so important to me and ask Him to take care of her situation. I realized that I was concerned that she might not be able to rest well if someone else was in the room and I wanted the best for her. I began to pray that she would get great care and all the rest she needed.

After her surgery, the surgeon told us that everything had gone extremely well and that she was being moved to a different room than had originally been planned for her. He looked at me and said, "I think you'll like it." I thought that was a bit odd, but I went with it!

We were taken to the 12th floor of the hospital, which I learned later, was designated for heads of state, foreign dignitaries, and royalty. As the elevator doors opened, we walked into what appeared to be the lobby of a five-star hotel. There were gorgeous, fragrant lilies in the lobby and a concierge! My daughter was taken to a room that was furnished with cherry wood bedroom furniture, a dining room table, and a living area.

Within a few minutes, there was a knock on the door and a butler entered the room with a crystal ice bucket and a leather-bound menu. Shortly thereafter, afternoon tea was served!

I couldn't believe my eyes! I had no idea that this type of room existed in a hospital! I learned a lot from this experience. Primarily, I learned that when you let go and let God, He will take care of your need – even in a way that you could not have even asked for! My daughter could not have gotten better care!

Helen Steiner Rice said it best, I think. "When you are in trouble and worried and sick at heart and your plans are upset and your world falls apart, remember God's ready and waiting to share the burden you find much too heavy to bear– So with faith, 'Let Go and Let God' lead your way into a brighter and less troubled day."

The Bible has a lot to say about this topic. One of my favorite passages is Matthew 6:26-30:

[26] *"Look at the birds of the air; they do not sow or reap or store away in barns, and yet your heavenly Father feeds them. Are you not much more valuable than they? [27] Can any one of you by worrying add a single hour to your life?*

[28] *And why do you worry about clothes? See how the flowers of the field grow. They do not labor or spin. [29] Yet I tell you that not even Solomon in all his splendor was dressed like one of these. [30] If that is how God clothes the grass of the field, which is here today and tomorrow is thrown into the fire, will he not much more clothe you—you of little faith?"*

Wow! Verse 27 hit me directly between the eyes – worrying doesn't add hours to our lives, it removes our joy.

You may be thinking, this is all well and good but how do we really do this? Here are some steps that may help.

First, pray about the situation that is causing your worry. Include God in this process. Tell Him what you want to let go of and ask Him to take it. Then wait on the Lord until you feel his presence – a peace that comes over you. Finally, leave what you have given him behind. When you find yourself worrying about it again remind yourself that you've given it to God. This is a lot easier said than done, especially by those who like to be in control, like me.

Some of my Bible Study friends and I were talking about this one day and they shared an exercise that they participated in that really drives "Letting Go and Letting God" home.

A wooden cross is placed on the ground. Each person in the group is given paper, a pen, and nails. Next, each person writes a worry or concern onto the paper and folds it in two. Each person then takes the paper or papers up to the cross. Using a hammer, the paper is then nailed to the cross and the person walks away. This is so powerful! I get goosebumps just thinking about it! We can literally take our worries to the cross and leave them there. Praise God!

Live in the Moment

What if we stopped thinking about the past and preparing for the future and just lived in the moment? This could have a huge impact on worry! Living in the moment is taking a moment in time to notice people, nature, a favorite song, or time with one of your favorite people. The key word here is notice.

My little grandson loves to be outside. He'd never come inside if he wasn't strongly encouraged by his mom and dad. A short while ago, my daughter mentioned that while they were outside a breeze started up. My little grandson stopped what he was doing, looked up and just smiled at the breeze for a second! He relished the breeze and then went back to playing. What a precious lesson from a 2-year-old! When my daughter told the story, she shared this scripture, "Be still, and know that I am God, I will be exalted among the nations, I will be exalted in the earth." (Psalm 46:10 NIV)

If you think about it, we won't ever get these moments back. So, join me and be present in each one.

Here are some of the moments I have noticed and treasure:

- ❖ The beautiful aroma of coffee brewing in the morning.
- ❖ A redbird making its way to the bird house on our front porch.
- ❖ My two-year-old grandson saying "Mia" for the first time. (This is my "grandmother" name)
- ❖ Birds singing in the morning.
- ❖ A ride in Gus (our Side-by-Side) with Buck.
- ❖ A phone conversation with my daughters and sisters.
- ❖ Lunch with my besties.
- ❖ Holding my first granddaughter (we have 6 grandsons) for the first time.
- ❖ Writing thank you notes – I get to relive the sweet gifts of friendship.
- ❖ Taking a hot shower.
- ❖ Listening to my favorite song on the radio.
- ❖ Learning about the accomplishments of my children and grandchildren.
- ❖ Writing a chapter that makes me smile.
- ❖ Fixing Thanksgiving Dinner.
- ❖ Looking at the lights on my Christmas tree.

- ❖ Learning how to navigate on a knee scooter (can I get an amen on this one!)

- ❖ Seeing a full moon over the water.

- ❖ Going to a pottery store and creating my first bowl!

- ❖ A cool breeze.

- ❖ The sound of the ocean.

- ❖ Watching my grandson play tennis.

- ❖ Baking and decorating cookies.

- ❖ Walking in the neighborhood with my girlfriends.

- ❖ Sitting on my front porch my rocking chair (this sounds just right for a gal who is 70!)

- ❖ Watching my daughter perform in the theater.

- ❖ Family birthday lunches/dinners.

- ❖ Playing cards with Buck.

- ❖ Listening to instrumental Christian music on YouTube.

- ❖ Attending our neighborhood ladies Bible Study.

- ❖ Reading a good mystery novel.

- ❖ Talking on the phone with my best friend.

- ❖ Hearing Buck practice special music for church.

- ❖ Sitting on the front porch watching the sunrise and drinking a cup of coffee.

❖ Taking opportunities to be kind to someone.

❖ Listening to Christian music as I scoot on down the road.

❖ Listening to my wind chimes on my back porch.

❖ Hearing my little grandson sing "The ABC's".

I could go on and on! Now, take a few minutes and jot down special moments. Savor them. Regardless of our circumstances, we can embrace each moment. Don't let them pass you by sweet sister.

My Special Moments

I'd love to hear about the moments you notice. Feel free to email me at <u>ruthwheat930@gmail.com</u>. Can't wait to connect!

Live today, let the past go, and let God take care of the future!

8

WORTH MORE THAN DIAMONDS

I've met women in their 60's, and then some, who feel as if their best life and what they had to offer was either nearing its end or over. I think that they may have had busy lives for so many years and when they slowed down, they began to question their value.

Consider this, we have at least 60 years under our belts filled with all kinds of knowledge and experiences. What if we shared this knowledge, these experiences, and our gifts with others? Great for us and great for them!

We were born with a life purpose. God chose to send us to earth at just the right moment in time and with the gifts we needed to live our life of purpose. This verse really drives this notion home: Psalm 139:13- Psalm 139:16.

13 "*For you created my inmost being;*

you knit me together in my mother's womb.

14 *I praise you because I am fearfully and wonderfully made;*

your works are wonderful,
I know that full well.

[15] *My frame was not hidden from you*
when I was made in the secret place,
when I was woven together in the depths of the earth.

[16] *Your eyes saw my unformed body;*
all the days ordained for me were written in your book
before one of them came to be."

Here's another example of how special we are. I found this phrase on a meme (you know, one of those Facebook pictures) and love it! I think it's just perfect for us!

"In my darkest days when I feel inadequate, unloved and unworthy, I remember whose daughter I am, and I straighten my crown".

Amen! As believers, we are daughters of Christ! I feel a bit like royalty right now. How about you? By the way, if you have a tiara, go get it and put it on! Be sure to notice how great you look with that sparkle on! Then, read on!

Okay, let's agree that we have a lot of worth. We've straightened our crowns, and we are ready to go. Sometimes, we have all the "willing and want to" and for some reason we get stuck. We get nervous and begin to think of all the reasons we can't do something. The evil one steps in and paralyzes us in the form of negative self-talk. Finding all the things wrong with us or things we can't do.

For example, harmful ideas such as I'm not good enough, I don't have a degree, I don't have the right personality, I'm not very smart, or I'm too quiet or too loud, can leave us believing that we don't really have a lot to offer.

We may also find ourselves thinking, my hair is too curly, too gray; I'm too fat or too thin. My eyes are too far apart, my nose is too big, I don't remember as much as I used to, I walk slower than everyone else, and so on! I could go on and on, but you get the picture! Our society sends a lot of signals our way that contribute to our feelings of inadequacy. We may buy into this and start judging ourselves very harshly.

Okay my friends, here's the deal. God created us in His image. He created us just the way we are. He knew us before we were born. He loved us so much that he sent His Son to die for us. That's how much we are valued!

The best way to let go of this negative self-talk is to ask God to highlight your attributes. Find something every day that you like about yourself and thank God for that gift.

Several years ago, one of my dearest friends, Brenda Vicente and I wrote a book entitled, "Help! My Wonder Woman Cape is Caught in the Vacuum!" Our goal with this book was to remind women to let go of the notion that they needed to be Wonder Woman and celebrate the wonderous woman they were created to be.

One of the exercises in the book encouraged women to write

down things that they appreciated about themselves. Many women shared that this wasn't necessarily an easy task. My niece said that she was having trouble, so she asked her boys what they liked about her. Their first response was her spaghetti! Then they went on to say things like her smile, her hugs, and so on. It's not always big, significant things that make us special to someone else.

God has given each of us a life's purpose. One of my favorite scriptures in the Bible is found in Esther. *"And who knows but that you have come to your royal position for such a time as this?"* Esther 4:14. This verse speaks to stepping up to fulfill God's purpose for our lives.

There is purpose in every moment we live.

You may be very clear on your life's purpose but if not, here are three steps to uncovering it.

❖ **Study God's Word.** Reading the stories of Esther, Ruth, and other women in the Bible brought clarity to my purpose. Other scriptures such as Jeremiah 29:11 *"For I **know** the **plans** I have for you,"* declares the Lord, *"**plans** to prosper you and not to harm you, **plans** to give you hope and a future."* were also instrumental to my discovering my purpose.

❖ **Pray for direction.** God created us. He has a plan for us. Talk to Him about His plan for you.

❖ **Draw on your God given passions.** As believers, we were given spiritual gifts on the day we accepted Jesus Christ as our Savior. I believe that these gifts drive our passions. I've learned that often when I am the most comfortable doing something, it's because I am doing something I love to do.

However, there are times that I **don't** feel comfortable doing something. Doubt sets in and though I feel God calling me to do it, I am hesitant. When this happens, I need to feel the fear and do it anyway. It's in these times, I need to quit trying to do something in my own strength and lean into His. This scripture is a great reminder that God's strength will deliver me. "*He gives strength to the weary and increases the power of the weak.*" Isaiah 40:29

What a blessing that we each have been given these spiritual gifts. If you haven't done a spiritual gifts assessment, check with your church to see what they may have available, or look for sources online that are helpful.

The bottom line is that we are beautiful women with a God-given purpose, and we are loved by our Father. And, we have a purpose to fulfill until we take our last breath.

Consider Elizabeth and Sarah. Elizabeth was 88 years old when she had John! Sarah was 90 years old when she had Isaac! God gave them the desires of their heart when they least expected it!

During this phase of our lives, we may find that we can have an even greater impact than we did when we were younger!

Take a look at these questions and jot down your thoughts.

❖ What are some of your gifts? Or what are things that you do really well?

❖ What is your life's purpose?

❖ How are the ways that you can live your life purpose?

9

ESTELLE

Early in the book, I introduced you to my mom, Kathleen Estelle Buras. The way she lived her life is evidence to me that life can be as busy we want to be, purpose driven and joyful no matter what the age.

Mom retired from a 30-year medical career and immediately went to work at a Lutheran Children's School. She became the administrative assistant there at age 65. She worked 3 days a week until she was 84. I asked her why she loved working there so much and she said, "I love giving hugs and Band-Aids to little ones." The only reason she stopped working is that our Father called her home.

I learned a lot from my mom. She was such a positive force. Here are some of the lessons she taught me.

One of my favorite lessons - Look for the Good and Think Positively- has served me well in my life. But it wasn't always so.

My mom saw the good in everyone and expected things to work

out. After a weekend of shopping in Arlington TX, where my sister Susan lived, we headed home back to Houston. I was the driver, and I hadn't paid any notice to the gas gauge. When I noticed that it gas gauge was indicating an empty tank, I freaked out! My mom said, "It will be okay. We'll find a gas station in time." Ya'll, I loved my mom, but that day her positivity was a bit maddening. In an outburst I said, "No, we won't! We don't have a clue where the next gas station is". This was before the days of GPS that can tell you where everything is from dog park to a hot dog stand.

I kept driving, noticing my mom praying silently and a miracle happened. A gas station appeared (seemingly out of nowhere). We coasted into the gas station on fumes, and a ton of embarrassment on my part. In my mother's wisdom, she didn't say I told you so. She simply said, "I think I'll go to the bathroom while we're here." Bless her heart!

As I mentioned earlier, I am one of five children. Growing up, we didn't have much money, but I never heard my mom complain. I can't remember one instance where she chose the negative over a positive in a situation. I'm sure she had her moments, but we didn't see them. She raised us to be color blind, to accept everyone through God's eyes, and to look for the positive in every situation.

My grandmother, Ruth Estelle Ragazinsky was the other driving force in my life. As the old saying goes, my mom and my grandmother were "cut from the same cloth". Two memories about my grandmother stand out in my mind. One happened when I was a toddler, and the other when I was about ten.

Grandma was always involved in church. She especially loved working with young people. One Tuesday night when she was visiting the kiddos in her Sunday School class, she met the sister of one of her students. Her name was Beverly. Grandma recognized that Beverly had special needs and asked where she attended Sunday School. Her parents replied that she didn't go, as there was no class for her. There was no mainstreaming back then.

After learning this, my grandmother was really convicted by the Holy Spirit. She felt that God was calling her to start a Sunday School class so that Beverly, and other children with special needs, had a place to go and learn to love Jesus.

She had no training, so she volunteered for an organization that served children with special needs. She recalled one of her favorite memories was dancing with the children to Elvis' "Blue Suede Shoes"!

And so, it began. As a result of her decision, children, and adults with all types of special needs had a chance to go to church and learn about God's love. She was asked to assist the Southern Baptist Convention in starting a ministry for special needs and help with the curriculum. She had no training, just a passion to do what God called her to do and the persistence to build the program from the ground up.

One of my favorite memories was the day she was given the Jefferson Award for community service in Houston, TX based upon her work with these children. What an accomplishment!

At 50, my grandmother decided that she wanted to be a nurse. So, she went to nursing school and became an LVN. She worked in the newborn nursery and was blessed to be able to care for three of her grandchildren when they were born.

Here's what I learned from my grandmother.

When God speaks, listen. You don't need to have experience to answer the call. A faith that God will give you what you need will see you through.

We are never too old to follow the desires of our heart. My grandmother didn't work outside the home, so when she announced that she was going to nursing school at 50, we said "Okay, then!" She went for it and never looked back!

10

GETTING' OLD AIN'T FOR SISSIES

Getting old ain't for sissies was a phrase that Nancy Wheat, Buck's mom, used in a conversation about some of the physical issues she was having. I met her when she was in her 90's. I loved her spunk, her wisdom, and her sense of humor. She lost the love of her life the year that I met her.

Nancy loved to sing, host amazing family Christmas parties, tell wonderful stories of raising Buck and his brother, Mike, and her life as a teacher. She always had a pot of coffee ready when anyone stopped to visit.

Quick witted, a passion for children, faithful to her Creator, a great cook, and tenacity were some of her characteristics, but "sissy" wasn't one of them. At 92 she was still driving and living on her own.

This is what I learned from Nancy.

❖ Regardless of any physical issues, we can find a way to live

61

joyous lives.

❖ 90 is the "new 60".

❖ Have faith that you can...

❖ Spending time sharing memories is really good for our souls.

❖ Put on a pot of coffee, you never know who might knock on your door.

❖ Make new memories, take advantage of every moment you have.

❖ Find joy in the smallest things.

I believe the biggest lesson I learned from her was not to let age define you. I've met ladies who subscribed to this mindset and those who didn't. Those that did seemed to enjoy life more.

Nancy certainly did believe this! Sadly, Nancy passed away a few months before Buck and I got married. She made such a difference in my life during the short time that I knew her. I believe my life is better for having her in it.

Finally, Nancy reminded me that when things get tough, pull up your big girl panties and move on!

11

I'M NOT OLD!

I choose not to use the term "old" as it relates to age. I prefer the word, "older". You may be wondering what difference it makes. I believe that our mindset changes when we use certain words or phrases. For example, the word "old" to me sounds 'worn out' or 'used up'. While I have days that I am worn out, I know I'm not used up! To me, the word "older" means that I've just increased in age. One of my favorite commercials on TV features an older woman who says, "Age is just a number, and mine is unlisted!" Love this!

I overheard Buck tell one of our friends that we weren't allowed to use the word "old" in our house. By golly, I think he gets it!

There are many phrases and words that we use as we age that can affect our mind set negatively. And when we have a negative mindset, we look at the world very differently. We feel defeated. Sadly, one of my friends, who focuses on all the things she can't do, said "I'm just waiting to die." I don't know about you sister, but I want to live every second of my life and slide into Heaven when it's time for me to go!

A couple of examples of phrases we might find ourselves saying are, "I can't do this anymore" and "Well you know, I'm not as young as I used to be". These phrases may cause us to think that we don't add value.

What if, we adjusted our thinking and changed these phrases to" I was able to do this...but now, I do this..." Or "I did that when I was younger, now I do this..." See the difference? One is I can't, the other is I can. Let's face it, there are things that our age, or physicality may keep us from doing that we may have done before.

I used to be able to run up and down stairs lickity split! Being able to navigate stairs that way really came in handy sometimes. Now, I walk up and down the stairs and hang onto the rail so that I don't fall. I still get where I'm going, though it may take a few more seconds to do so.

Okay, how do we overcome a negative mindset? Here are some ideas:

- ❖ Ask God to shine His light on all your blessings! It's pretty difficult to be negative when your see what God has done and is doing in your life.

- ❖ Surround yourself with positivity. Seek out positive influences in your life. Spend time with supportive and optimistic people who uplift you. And limit your time around negative people! They can be exhausting! Do things that bring you joy and make you feel good about yourself. Stay away from too much negative news!

❖ Take care of your physical health – there's a strong connection between physical and mental well-being. Get plenty of sleep and exercise. Take care of yourself – it will have a positive effect on your mood.

❖ Practice self-compassion. Treat yourself with kindness and understanding. Avoid being self-critical, it will never bring you joy. Our Father created us in His image. We are exactly as we need to be. We are beautiful in His sight.

My friend, consider focusing on what you can do in your life versus what you can't do! It will make your heart happy! Remember, we aren't old! We are well-seasoned!

Take a few minutes and jot down some things you "can" do. Then celebrate them!

12

WHAT DO YOU SAY? THANK YOU!

"What do you say? Thank you!" Boy, if I heard this from my mom once, I heard it a million times! My mom was a stickler on saying "Thank you." And guess what? I followed in my mother's footsteps and asked the same "What do you say?" question to my kiddos.

Acknowledging my appreciation became second nature to me. Typically, I was grateful for something a friend, teacher or family member had done for me.

I met a gal about 8 years ago that really believed in the benefits of our being grateful. This piqued my interest, so I began studying the subject. Through my research I learned that being grateful is good for our spirits and our health! For one thing, it's impossible to be unhappy when you're grateful! I also learned that when I started my day with gratitude, my day was better!

Here are some ideas to help create an attitude of gratitude:

❖ Reflect on those things for which you are grateful. There

are so many things we can name. And most important, eternal life – Jesus giving his life so that we could be saved.

Our blessings are many! Get yourself a beautiful journal and write down 2 or 3 things for which you are grateful each day. Creating this gratitude journal will only take a few minutes, but it will impact your day in a positive way! Some days, you may feel like your "gratitude juices" aren't flowing. You're grateful for sure, but you feel like you need a little kickstart.

My friend, Sue, shared a gratitude practice that she did with her children. They made their gratitude list using words that started with the alphabet. For example, they would write "I'm grateful for..."

- A – Aunt Alice making a delicious lunch on Sunday

- B – Breakfast this morning

- C – Church – a church where we can worship God.

What a great idea! I'm going use this when I get stuck!

❖ Share your gratitude journal entries with others. How about sending a text to a family member or friend that lists what you're grateful for? Encourage them to do the same. This daily practice can have such a positive effect on your day-to-day activities, and it deepens relationships.

❖ Praise God for His blessings – Blessings come in all shapes and sizes. A blessing could be as simple as a day filled with sunshine! Ephesians 1:3 tells us that God the Father has *"blessed us in Christ with every spiritual blessing"*. James 1:17 says, *"Every good and perfect gift is from above, coming down from the Father of lights."*

❖ When things get tough, stop for a moment, and think about the things you're grateful for. It may not change the circumstances, but it will be beneficial to get through the tough times. One thing for certain, we can be grateful that our Father is holding us through these times.

❖ Send a thank you note to someone. I prefer a handwritten note to email or texting, but how you do it is not as important as getting it done. Not only is this good for your spirit; but think about how this will make the recipient feel! This little act of gratitude can have a huge impact on people.

❖ Set aside a "No-complain" day. Wow! This might be quite an undertaking! What a difference this can make in how you go through your day. It will have a positive effect on your spirit.

The following page has some space for you to get started on your gratitude practice. Jot down a minimum of 3 things you're grateful for.

I'm grateful for...

1.
2.
3.

Now, get yourself a pretty journal and capture your thoughts every day! It will do your heart good!

By the way, I'm writing this chapter in June in Huntsville, TX. We've been averaging over 90 degrees each day. And, we have tons of humidity! I am so grateful for William Carrier - he invented air conditioning!

I feel so blessed that you have chosen to read this book! If you need a "Gratitude Buddy" and want to share what you're grateful for, I'm your girl! Just send me an email at ruthwheat930@gmail.com and I'll share mine with you!

Before you go to the next chapter, consider this... *"Folks are usually about as happy as they make their minds up to be."* Abraham Lincoln

13

I HAVE EXTRA TIME! NOW WHAT?!

As women in our 60's+ we may find that we have more time on our hands than we did in our 40's and 50's. During those years, we may have found ourselves thinking, "I would really love to have some more time to do things!" Now that we have arrived, we may wonder what to do with our time. I know I did.

A friend of mine told me that when she retired, she was busier than when she was working! Wow! That's crazy! Right? Maybe not...she actually found that she was able to dive into things she always wanted to do.

Let's look at that notion. I imagine that most of us have had ideas of things we'd love to do but they had to be put on the back burner because we had other priorities. I say, we need to put those on our front burner and start getting them done! It's never too late to start! Here we go!!

Here are some ideas to get you going...

1. Start, or complete, your bucket list. A bucket list is comprised of things that you'd love to do. You can put anything you'd like on your list. A couple of years ago, I decided that I wanted to hold a little monkey. They're so cute and just like little babies. So, when Buck and I went on a cruise, we booked an excursion to a monkey sanctuary, and I got to hold a Capuchin monkey. Oh, my goodness! So much fun! By the way, Buck has put his foot down against getting a monkey!

2. Pursue the desires of your heart. Identify your passions. Consider the activities that genuinely ignite your enthusiasm. What are the hobbies and interests or causes do you feel strongly about? Also, pay attention to the activities that make you lose track of time, as well as those that bring a sense of purpose and meaning to your life.

   I love to make people smile. One way I do this is by decorating sugar cookies. I really enjoy giving them to people and it is so satisfying to see the delight on the faces of the folks eating them!

   Another way I like to make people smile is by creating memorable retreats for ladies! I'm a partner in a retreat ministry called "Girls Just Wanna Retreat" and we get to create these memories often! By the way, I make sure there are plenty of cookies!

   Helen Keller said it best – "One can never consent to creep when one feels the impulse to soar!"

3. Try new experiences! Step out of your comfort zone and be open to new things. Even if they feel a little uncomfortable. Take a class, travel, or volunteer. Recently, I was on my way to town, and I saw a sign that advertised Square Dance lessons! I think Buck and I need to give that a try!

4. Set some goals! Write them down! And, if you really want to get crazy, tell a friend. Then, you're kind of obligated! For example, I have a weight loss goal that I set to reach this year – I'm feeling a bit too fluffy! What goals do you have? They can be anything! When you reach them, be sure to celebrate!

5. Take action! Giddy up girl! You gotta get started!

Here's a story that may give you some inspiration! I ran across this story in "Everyday Health" by Mike Dolan while I was doing research for this book. It's an excerpt from an article entitled "10 Women Over 60 Who Inspire Wellness and Living Your Best Life."

Diana Nyad set a world record by swimming 102 miles from the Bahamas to Florida at age 30. She became an overnight sensation. However, she was so tired of training for years in the pool, she decided to quit swimming and pursue broadcasting. She was very successful with her career.

When Diana turned 60, a dream that she had when she was younger, resurfaced. When she was 29, she tried and failed to make the swim from Cuba to the United States. Could she battle ocean currents, box jellyfish, and even sharks to do it now?"

Diana went back to grueling training sessions, spending 13 hours at a time training for her dream. She attempted 4 times without success. The fifth time was a charm. At 65, she completed the 110-mile swim from Havana to Key West, something that no other swimmer has been able to accomplish!

This is an amazing story that illustrates our ability to tackle things at any age.

What is your dream? What would you like to do? It doesn't have to be as grandiose as swimming 110 miles, for sure. Be quiet and listen to your heart. Then, take a few minutes to jot down your thoughts here...

My dreams:

| |
| |
| |
| |
| |
| |
| |

14

LIFE IS NOT PERFECT,
BUT IT CAN BE BEAUTIFUL!

Patti Kaye Jones is my precious sister. She has three beautiful adult children – two daughters and a son. She married her high school sweetheart, Steve, and they began their lives together 47 years ago.

She had difficulty with all three of her pregnancies, but God saw her through each one. Her youngest, a son was born prematurely with cerebral palsy. Raising a child with this condition is difficult and can be heartbreaking at times. She would tell you that her life is beautiful. Here's her story.

Jeremiah, her youngest, was born on July 4, 1988. After having two daughters, they were excited to have a boy! It was evident that Jeremiah was born with some difficulties, but what a beautiful baby!

In addition to Jeremiah having cerebral palsy, he also was autistic and only had peripheral vision. Even after surgery to straighten his legs, in an effort to walk, he was unable to do so.

Raising a child with special needs is difficult, but oh so rewarding. Patti told me one day that they focused on what Jeremiah could do, instead of what he couldn't do.

He could sing! He could pray! He could hold hands with her and love her! One of my favorite pictures is of Patti and Jeremiah putting socks in a box to send to a child in need and then praying for the child that was to receive it.

Jeremiah has such a tender heart. When he sings hymns, he tears up on some of his favorites.

Recently, Patti posted this on Facebook. "We are blessed by God's gift of our son Jeremiah! What joy he brings to us every day! God has used Jeremiah to teach us so many things! His determination to do everyday things that we don't even think about amazes us each day! We love you, Jeremiah Caleb Jones!"

I share this story for two reasons. The first is that God's gift of Jeremiah to our family has taught us that each of us, regardless of our abilities, has a gift and can make a huge difference in the world around us.

The second is the rest of the story...

In addition to caring for a special needs son, Patti is an amazing chef and homemaker. She has gotten on the saddle of a horse and helped her husband round up cattle. This activity blows my "city girl" mind! Ya'll she even looks cute in full camo outfits!

As an amazing gardener she raises vegetables, and boy are they yummy! I love the pictures she shares with those beautiful vegetables front and center!

Patti has taught children's church in so many creative ways. She has fed cowboys getting ready to work, held ladies Bible studies in her home, and she and her husband hosted Wednesday night Bible study in their home.

Patti is 66 at the writing of this book and is one of the strongest women I know. Regardless of her circumstances, which can be difficult at times, she wakes each day with gratitude and a desire to serve the Lord every day, no matter what!

Even though I am her older sister, she has really inspired me. She's taught me so many lessons. I am so grateful that God placed her in our family. She definitely follows in both of the "Estelle's" footsteps.

Though we might never find ourselves in Patti's situation, we do have trials that sometimes seem insurmountable. Lean on our Father God and know that life can be beautiful when you love the Lord and thank Him for the life you've been given.

15

LIVING A MAVIS LIFE

This chapter title may seem a bit quirky, after all, who is Mavis? Hang on, I'll fill you in.

Mavis was my little rescue dog. For years, I purchased pure bred Yorkies (Yorkshire Terriers) from breeders. They were precious little lap dogs that just made my heart sing. Both of my little Yorkies died, having lived 11 years each.

After Maddie, my second Yorkie, died I decided that I would wait awhile and decide whether I wanted to get another sweet little dog. My heart had been broken twice and I wasn't sure I had it in me to try again. My sweet little grandson knew how my heart hurt and suggested that maybe I should go with a parrot because they could be annoying and perhaps, I wouldn't love it as much! In his sweet, tender way, he was trying to find a way to minister to me.

God knew that I needed to love a little dog again, so the urge built up inside me. I was recently divorced. I felt lonely, so I decided to move forward. You know there is just something so joyous about having an opportunity to pour our love into something so precious!

I told my friends that I was on the lookout for a breeder and Mary Margaret, my sister from another mother, suggested that I adopt a rescue instead. She convinced me that there was just the perfect little baby out there that needed me.

I contacted a group that rescued small dogs, Tiny Paws. They were excited to hear from me, and after speaking to them, I knew this was the route I needed to take.

They directed me to their website so that I could look at the pictures and descriptions of the dogs available for adoption. Ya'll, this site reminds me of Match.com! (remember, that's where I met Buck!)

As I was going through the pages, my eyes and my heart landed on a sweet little Yorkie/Chinese Crested mixed breed. She was black and looked like my other Yorkies with the exception of a large tuft of hair on the top of her head. Her name was Mavis. I learned that Mavis had been found near a day care center, hair matted, dirty and no collar.

The sweet lady that found her was a hair stylist, so she took her to her salon, gave her a bath, brushed her fur, and trimmed and painted her nails. Her next act of love was to get her to Tiny Paws.

I met with the foster parents, spent time playing with Mavis, and in a few short days, I learned I was approved to adopt her. What joy!

I share this story with you for a couple of reasons. One is that Mavis's story reminds me of how we come to God a hot mess, and yet He believes we are beautiful. And second, I wanted to share what I learned from Mavis. I think her characteristics are ones that we can embody to love life BIG!

Mavis weighed 6 pounds. She was a little bitty thing with a huge personality. Her size didn't stop her – she BELIEVED she was big! Here are a few of her characteristics that I believe we can strive for in our lives. There is no age limit on them!

Excited about little things – Have you ever noticed how excited a dog gets when playing with a favorite toy or a ball? They get a hold of it and shake it seemingly for hours. What could our lives be like if we took joy in small things? A beautiful sunny day, a phone call from a friend, a funny post on Facebook, or watching our favorite TV show? All the little things add up and we experience joy in a big way.

Always up for an adventure – It seemed like every time I'd walk in a room or get up from the couch, Mavis would run over to my feet and look at me expectantly. She was ready to go do whatever was next! Let's look for adventures to enjoy. Adventures can be big or small. Sometimes just getting a pedicure is an adventure for me! Look for opportunities and grab some gals to go with you! It will make your heart happy!

Persistence – Mavis sat in the window in our living room during the day. I believe she thought she was in charge of the street! Anyway, something would catch her eye and she would bark - a lot! Even if whatever she saw was no longer there - she kept at it until at some point she felt finished. Persistence plays a big role in our feeling like we are accomplishing things.

Things may be a little more difficult to do as we age, and we may feel like giving up sometimes. This is just when our persistence needs to kick in. We may not do things the same way, but we can get things done.

Making the best of a bad situation - Little dogs like Yorkies tend to have joint problems and Mavis was no exception. I noticed one day that she was limping and favoring her right leg. We made an appointment with her vet and learned that she needed a knee replacement. That tiny little knee needed to be fixed so that she could live her best life.

We had the knee replacement done and Mavis, wearing the dreaded "cone of shame", quickly learned that she had to take things easy. We did all the required physical therapy and Mavis was a trooper. She did beautifully and in a few weeks, she was good to go. Mavis started running and never looked back!

A year or so after that experience, I noticed her limping again. I was so concerned that we might need to go through another knee replacement! I was not ready for that experience again.

After a quick visit with the vet, I learned that she had contracted some type of infection in her little toe, and it had to be removed.

I was worried how losing her toe would impact her gait. The vet, who has a great sense of humor, told me not to worry. He said, "She won't be able to play the piano like she used to, but she'll be fine." Oh, my goodness, he knew exactly how to calm my nerves with laughter.

Once her paw healed, she started running! She didn't let the fact that she only had 4 toes stop her!

I learned by watching Mavis that we have to accept things as they come and do what we can to move forward. Then, when we get past the tough situation – Celebrate! And - RUN!

I could go on for hours about my little Mavis, can you tell? Mavis died in 2022. Her little heart gave out. I like to think that she just used it up loving everyone.

We had her cremated and the folks at the vet made an imprint of her little paw as a keepsake. The imprint was of the paw with only 4 toes! I don't think that they intentionally selected that paw but I'm really glad they did. I believe it is the perfect way to remember her spirit!

I hope that your heart was touched by her story and that you've got some food for thought.

Let's live a Mavis life.

16

WOMEN AND LEGACY

Lois and Eunice are two Biblical characters about whom little is known. What is known is that they, as a grandmother and mother, had a significant impact on Timothy's life, one of the missionary Paul's cherished friends. What did they do? They shared their faith with him as a child and saw him grow into a godly man who shared the gospel on missionary journeys.

In 2 Timothy 1:5 Paul mentions these women "*I am reminded of your sincere faith, which first lived in your grandmother **Lois** and in your mother **Eunice** and, I am persuaded, now lives in you also.*"

2 Timothy 3:14-15 says, "*You, however, continue in the things you have learned and become convinced of, knowing from who you have learned them, and that from childhood you have known the sacred writings which are able to give you the wisdom that leads to salvation through faith which is in Christ Jesus.*"

As daughters of Christ, we have the opportunity, and

responsibility, to leave a faith-filled legacy within our own families and the lives of others.

Let me introduce you to three ladies who remind me so much of Lois and Eunice – Barbara, Carolyn, and Pat.

These precious ladies are dear friends that go to my church (Carolyn is also my neighbor and walking buddy.) I knew when I met them, that they were something special!

After getting to know them, I felt led to share some of their stories, their zest for life and their relationship with Jesus Christ with you. At the time of this writing, Pat is 89, Carolyn is 83, and Barbara is 82.

I'd also like to share my sister, Mary Helen's story with you. Though her story is a bit different, I think you'll agree that she mirrors the hearts of Lois and Eunice.

Meet Barbara

Barbara, also known as Bobbie, is so much fun! I have a special fondness for her because we are both short girls! I love her spunk and great sense of humor! There are a lot of pastors, past and present, in Barbara's family, so her life has been infused with God's message of hope. She has had to lean on that promise as she experienced breast cancer (she's healed, praise God!) and experiencing the sorrow of being widowed twice. The experiences could certainly bring a gal down, but Barbara took her own advice to "give everything to God" and was able to weather storms.

The Huntsville Sheriff's Department got quite a gal when Barbara joined the force. She loved serving the community and as to being an officer, she said, "it gets in your blood!" Barbara put a lot of hours in at the Sheriff's Department, working in the office during the week and out in the community on the weekend. However, she made sure never to miss church!

I asked Barbara to share some advice on living a full life and she said,

- "Don't behave - it's boring!" We had a good belly laugh over this one! She's right! Sometimes we take ourselves too seriously, girls!

- "Put God first, everything will fall into place."

- Her final piece of advice was to "stay active!" She gets up early and walks a mile and a half every day! You go girl!

Remember Lois and Eunice? Barbara definitely reminds me of them. Barbara's husband died and left her with a young son. Through God's guidance, her influence and her example, her son became the Chief of the Huntsville Police Department and is a beloved Bible teacher at our church. What a beautiful legacy!

Meet Carolyn

My goodness! Have you ever met someone who is quiet spoken with rock-solid faith? This statement epitomizes my friend, Carolyn.

My friendship with Carolyn is a double blessing. She lives up the hill from me and we go to church together. As a matter of fact, my husband and I first visited our church because Carolyn invited us!

Carolyn was raised in a Methodist church, her uncle, and brothers both being pastors. She became a Christian at a young age and loved studying about Jesus.

After marrying, Carolyn and her husband joined a church that, she came to know later, didn't really speak to the love of God, focusing mainly on man-made rules about living one's life.

After leaving the congregation, Carolyn leaned on her faith and became a devoted learner of the scriptures. She calls herself a "life-long" learner.

As a wife and mother to four children, Carolyn has spent her life caring for her family. She's been through many trials, but her faith has kept her going. She has such a servant's heart and is a HUGE prayer warrior!

When I asked Carolyn to share her thoughts about living a purpose-filled life, she said,

- ❖ "Keep in daily contact with God – study His word."
- ❖ "Be thankful and praise God for all your blessings."
- ❖ "Keep doing!"
- ❖ "Never give up hope and enjoy the things you are still able to do at our age."
- ❖ "Don't dwell on the past, look to the future!"

Carolyn's likeness to Lois and Eunice is evidenced by her daughter, who with her husband, raised children who love Jesus and are passing that legacy onto her children.

Every now and again, Carolyn will say, "I wish I was more outgoing." But, oh, her quiet witness and love for the Lord speaks volumes! And she'll be the first gal when she meets a new neighbor to invite them to our neighborhood ladies Bible study. We need lots of "Carolyn's" in our world!

Meet Pat

Pat is full of life and love for the Lord. She is the pianist at our church, and oh, how I love to hear her tickle those ivories! Oh, by the way, she has been a member of our church for 49 years!

Pat met her husband, Gene, through the efforts of Gene's sister and her friend, Barbara. (You met her earlier.) Pat was quite the catch, in fact, Gene mentioned marriage only two weeks after meeting her! You know, when God sends you "The One", you just know, right?

Pat married Gene a couple of years later. After they married, Gene accepted God's call (one that he received at age 16) to go into ministry. Actually, Gene asked Pat if she would ever consider being a pastor's wife before he accepted God's call. She replied by saying that she thought she could and that launched a ministry that touched many lives.

God blessed Pat and Gene with two sons and then heartache

struck - their baby girl was stillborn. Pat told me that those days were so dark, and she was only able to get through those times with her faith in God.

Barbara says that Pat was the perfect preacher's wife! She loved on people in Jesus' name even when they showed up at their home sometimes in the middle of the night! Because she and Gene had experienced such heartache, they were able to minister to others in their times of struggles and grief.

Pat and Gene were married 55 years and then God called Gene home. He was the pastor of our little church in Huntsville TX for 29 years. Another devasting heartbreak for Pat, but she found comfort in her growing family and in God's love and grace.

At 86, (did you catch that?! 86!) Pat decided to retire from managing the office at the storage company that she and Gene owned. Today, she plays the piano every day, a passion that she developed in the third grade, and tends to the upkeep of her garden and home. Boy! She grows the best tasting cherry tomatoes!

I asked Pat to share her thoughts about how she lives such a full life, and this is what she said,

- ❖ "I stay mentally alert!"
- ❖ "I keep busy doing things that I love such as making photo albums from the thousands of family pictures that I've collected through the years."
- ❖ "I put God first - He makes everything right!"

❖ "I'm grateful for every new day! It gives me another day to live my wonderful life."

Pat has another calling; she single-handedly makes sure that every visitor to our church receives a warm smile and a huge welcome!

Her "Lois and Eunice" legacy is her multi-generational family. From the adults to the children, they are all active in their respective churches and her grandson is a pastor, just like his grandfather!

Meet Mary Helen

Mary Helen, lovingly known as "H" to our family, is my Irish twin. We were both born in the same year – January and December. We've had some fun with that through the years, most importantly because of Mary Helen's sense of humor.

Mary Helen's story is a bit different from Barbara, Carolyn, and Pat's in that she has never married and doesn't have children of her own. Though not being called to be a mother, she was called to bring the love of Jesus to little ones through her activities at church.

Mary Helen has taught pre-school Sunday School classes for over 40 years. She's so clever with how to create an application to the Bible story so that her little ones can receive the message. I can't tell you how many times I've asked her what she's up to and would get answers like "I'm looking for some raisins to put on celery and peanut butter logs so that it looks like ants are crawling on them."

This may have been during the story of Noah and all of the creatures that were on the Ark with him. She's made these wonderful Bible stories come to life for the little students.

Mary Helen acquired a heart for spreading God's word when she was a teenager in a girls' missions group sponsored by our church. She carried that passion into adulthood and became a leader in the same girls' missions' group. She was a leader in this group for over 30 years ministering to hundreds of young women.

Having such a heart for missions, she dreamt of going to Africa on a mission trip. She realized that dream in her late 50's! I wish you could see the smile on her face when she shares her experience in Kenya. One of her favorite memories was listening to the children singing "Jesus Loves Me." I'm so grateful that God gave her the opportunity to leave some of her heart in Africa.

Animal costumes, construction paper, glitter, glue, funny noise makers, balloon animals, and puzzles are just some of the items that can be found in her storage closets. Known by all as the "fun one" you can always count on her to make sure that all gatherings include laughter!

All of the children and grandchildren in our family love "H". She is their prayer warrior, shows up for plays, sports events, and activities that they are in. What a blessing she is!

She has built a "Lois and Eunice" legacy in her life that has impacted countless young women and children's lives with her love for Jesus. Many of her "kids" have gone on to be in church leadership positions.

Today, Mary Helen is 69 and still teaching 4-year-olds in Sunday School! What amazes me is that she can get up and down off the floor when she's playing with them! That's a feat for me on one of my best days!

What Legacy Do You Want to Leave?

Several years ago, I heard a speaker talk about our life legacy. She mentioned that one of the best exercises that we can do is to mentally take ourselves to our 100th birthday and consider what we want people to say about us as they go around the room. Though this may feel a bit self-serving, it's really an exercise to determine how you want to live your life and what your legacy can be.

For example, I want someone to say that I am kind. This desire drives me to be as kind as I can be to others which may include simply smiling and making eye contact with a stranger. (Now, Buck Wheat would tell you that I don't stop there – I can strike up a conversation with anyone!)

I also want to be known as someone who loves the Lord and seeks His purpose for my life. This desire drives me to live a life where people can see Jesus in me.

I could go on and on, but I really would like to give you an opportunity to spend a few minutes thinking about your 100th birthday and what you'd like to hear about your life. Take a little time and write down some of your thoughts here.

My 100th Birthday thoughts...

As I finish this chapter, I've taken some time to reflect on how I might improve on my own Lois and Eunice legacy. I have precious grandchildren who would love to sit in my lap while I read Bible stories to them. I can also spend more time, sharing what God has done for me within my family and friends. Perhaps I could take a young woman to lunch and treat her to a listening ear. Lots to do! I'd better get busy!

Giddy up!

17

LAUGH OUT LOUD

How long has it been since you've had a good belly laugh? I'm not talking about a chuckle; I'm talking about laughing so hard your sides hurt!

I love to laugh and really appreciate those with a good sense of humor. My sister Susan had such a contagious laugh and sometimes she laughed so hard she had to stop to catch her breath!

Laughter can be so good for us. There are many medical sources and journals that agree on the benefits of laughter. Here are just a few.

❖ Laughter enhances our intake of oxygen-rich air, stimulates our hearts, lungs, and muscles, and increases the endorphins that are released by your brain. These endorphins help our bodies avoid pain and increase feelings of pleasure.

❖ A belly laugh fires up and then cools down your stress

response, and it can increase and then decrease your heart rate and blood pressure. The result? A good, relaxed feeling.

❖ Laughter can also stimulate our circulation and aid in muscle relaxation, both of which can help reduce some of the physical symptoms of stress.

You may be thinking, there's a lot of stuff going on in our world that's not funny! You're right! I took a break from writing a few minutes ago and took a quick look at the news. Not the best idea! I heard and saw things that broke my heart. So, I decided I needed to get away from the news and do some laughing. I came upstairs and went straight to YouTube, my "go-to" place for lots of laughter.

Jeanne Robertson is one of my favorite comedians. She passed away in 2021, but gratefully, we have access to all of her videos on her website, JeanneRobertson.com, and YouTube. My all-time favorite show is entitled "Don't Send a Man to the Grocery Store." It doesn't matter how many times I watch it; I enjoy lots of belly laughs!

Another favorite is Chondra Pierce, a Christian comedian who really tickles my funny bone. She really relates to women and when she is telling a story, I'm right there with her! You can find her on YouTube, and you can purchase her videos on Amazon.

There are so many wonderful ways to enjoy laughter, and it is a choice. We laugh spontaneously at day-to-day things, but if we want to make sure we get some good laughs in on a regular basis, we need to take some action.

Remember those wonderful old sitcoms? My very favorite is "I Love Lucy." I have watched so many of those shows, and they are still funny! One of my favorites is Lucy working in the chocolate factory stuffing chocolates in her mouth, her hat and apron pockets!

There is a treasure trove of those "good old shows" that were good clean fun. Get out your remote and find your favorites and spend time laughing! It will do your heart good!

Need another idea for laughter? Here goes – Check out funny quotes on menopause! Girls, we have all been there and can totally relate!

I don't know about you, but I remember days that I would be all dolled up with great make up on, and in an instant I'd have a hot flash that would result in others staring in amazement as I started sweating profusely, and as a result, all that beautiful make up started melting!

There are a lot of funny quotes on the Internet! One of my favorites is "Next mood swing in 6 minutes! Be afraid, be very afraid!" (Courtesy of "livecool.com")

I believe one of my favorite ways to laugh is to go down memory lane and re-live some of the shenanigans I found myself in. I have two friends that I can safely say have shared some "Lucy and Ethel" moments with me.

Pam, one of my lifelong friends, and I found ourselves "dumpster diving" for some files that were missing from our office. We even put on maid's uniforms and the whole nine yards, to achieve our objective. Sadly, we didn't find the files, but we sure have laughed about this crazy experience throughout our friendship.

Brenda, a dear friend of over 20 years, and I found ourselves in a rainstorm in Tuscaloosa, Alabama trying to get to the apartment we were leasing for work. We drove through the storm and were so grateful when we found "home." We got out of the car, ran in the rain, got completely soaked and landed safely on the front porch. Brenda tried the key, and it didn't work. We were so confused! We tried again to no avail. We finally figured out that we were at the wrong apartment. (In our defense, they all looked the same!) So, we ran back into the storm and tried again. Gratefully, the second time was a charm!

I'll bet you've got some shenanigans on your memory lane! Take a minute, relive the moment, and laugh out loud!

Here's another idea! Call up one of your girlfriends and watch a funny show together! Put your phone on speaker and enjoy! My family does this at Christmas time with "Christmas Vacation." It's so much fun to laugh with others!

I ran across a statistic on a blog entitled Aging Healthily, Happily and Youthfully. It stated that the average 4-year-old laughs 300 times a day! The average 40-year-old, only 4. I'm not sure that this is scientifically proven, but we can safely say that children laugh a lot more than adults.

Children find joy in the smallest things. They delight in little wins and are typically happy, bringing lots of smiles to their little faces. Obviously, they get sad when they don't get their way, a trait that we often hang onto into adulthood. However, when I'm around my sweet ones, I see their joy and so enjoy listening to them laugh. It makes my heart sing.

So, ladies, let's bring back that little 4-year-old in us and laugh. It will do our hearts good!

Giddy up!

18

GIDDY UP!

Whew! You did it! You're almost finished with this book! I hope you've gotten lots of food for thought. We've covered a lot of ground. We've got so much living to do! It really doesn't matter how many more years we live, what matters is how we "live" in the years we have left.

So, you may be thinking what's next? How do I go about putting "Giddy Up" in my life? How about a To Do checklist? I don't know about you, but I have SO much information in my brain, I find I need to write things down to be sure that I take care of them. Can I get an "Amen!" sister?!

Because of all of this information, I find it's much easier when I use checklists!

How about a To Do list that will help us live and love our lives? I put one together based upon the suggestions you've read in the book, and I've included some spaces to write your own ideas. Check off the ones that you want to commit to and Giddy Up!

I hope you enjoy this To Do list. There are some blank spaces for you to use as you jot down all the things you want to do!

Giddy Up Estelle! To Do List

- ☐ Jot down your life experiences and share with others.
- ☐ Include activities into your life that support your life purpose.
- ☐ Consider lessons learned. How might they benefit others?
- ☐ Try something new on your life "Chacouterie Board."
- ☐ Be open to God's surprises. Look for them in the most unusual circumstances.
- ☐ Choose Joy
- ☐ Give your worries to God. Remember, He's got this!
- ☐ Notice moments and jot them down!
- ☐ Look for the good in all situations.
- ☐ Embrace being older and celebrate the life you have!
- ☐ Start a Gratitude Journal and write down your blessings!
- ☐ Try new experiences! Dream!
- ☐ Live a Mavis life!

Giddy Up Estelle! To Do List

- ☐ Consider those things that make your life beautiful. Jot them down!
- ☐ Write down the legacy for which you want to be remembered. Take action steps as needed.
- ☐ Infuse opportunities for laughter into you life.
- ☐ Get yourself a beautiful journal and make lots of notes!
- ☐ Remember, you're the daughter of a King! Celebrate your uniqueness!
- ☐
- ☐
- ☐
- ☐
- ☐
- ☐
- ☐
- ☐

Giddy Up Estelle! To Do List

☐
....

☐
....

☐
....

☐
....

☐
....

☐
....

☐
....

☐
....

☐
....

☐
....

☐
....

☐
....

☐
....

Let me know if you'd like to print a copy outside the book! I'm happy to send you one! ruthwheat930@gmail.com

19

DAILY JOURNAL

Some of the ideas shared in these chapters will be easier to implement if you use a daily journal. Writing things down such as your blessings, your daily goals or to do list, any thoughts that you'd like to capture and specific requests for prayer can be a great way to stay focused on living your best life.

A sample journal page is located on the next page. Feel free to copy and use. If you'd like to have a copy of the "Daily Journal" to use outside of the book, please contact me at and I'll be happy to send you a copy.

Happy Journaling!

Daily Journal

Day ——————————————————— Date: ————

Things that I am grateful for:

Things to do:

My prayer list:

Moments that made me happy:

20

FINAL THOUGHTS

Girl, I don't want to let you go! I'm imagining you reading this book in an "oh so comfy" spot with your favorite beverage nearby. I hope you've enjoyed the read and that your life is blessed in some way.

Here are some final thoughts to tuck into your heart:

- ❖ God has blessed us with His love, His grace, and the longevity of our lives.

- ❖ We were beautifully created in His image.

- ❖ We are daughters of a King.

- ❖ We have gifts to share.

- ❖ We have a purpose to live until we take our final breath.

- ❖ Laughter is the best medicine.

- ❖ We can make a difference in others' lives.

- ❖ God is the foundation of our joy and holds us in the palms of His hands.

❖ Our lives are not perfect, but they can be beautiful.

❖ We are promised that we don't need to worry. He's got this!

Let's Giddy up and live our best lives!

ABOUT THE AUTHOR

Ruth Wheat lives in Huntsville, Texas with her husband Buck and dog Pepper. She loves all the roles she's been given to play – wife, mother, Mia, Bible study leader, author, retreat planner and cookie baker. Her most treasured title is Daughter of Christ.

Made in the USA
Columbia, SC
04 December 2024

47340846R00061